THE
ULTIMATE

garden journal

This journal belongs to:

....

THE
ULTIMATE

garden journal

wishlist

PLANT/SEED	COST	COMPANY	NOTES

seed inventory

CROP	VARIETY	COMPANY	EXPIRES	QUANTITY

seed inventory

CROP	VARIETY	COMPANY	EXPIRES	QUANTITY

	Jan	Feb	Mar	Apr	May	Jun

at a Glance

Jul	Aug	Sep	Oct	Nov	Dec

Seasonal Checklist: *winter*

- .... ☐
- .... ☐
- .... ☐
- .... ☐
- .... ☐
- .... ☐
- .... ☐
- .... ☐
- .... ☐
- .... ☐
- .... ☐
- .... ☐

Seasonal Checklist: *spring*

- ☐
- ☐
- ☐
- ☐
- ☐
- ☐
- ☐
- ☐
- ☐
- ☐
- ☐
- ☐

Seasonal Checklist: Summer

- _____ ☐
- _____ ☐
- _____ ☐
- _____ ☐
- _____ ☐
- _____ ☐
- _____ ☐
- _____ ☐
- _____ ☐
- _____ ☐
- _____ ☐
- _____ ☐

Seasonal Checklist: autumn

- .... ☐
- .... ☐
- .... ☐
- .... ☐
- .... ☐
- .... ☐
- .... ☐
- .... ☐
- .... ☐
- .... ☐
- .... ☐
- .... ☐

Garden Plan

Garden Plan

Garden Plan

Garden Plan

Garden Plan

Garden Plan

Garden Plan

Garden Plan

Garden Plan

Garden Plan

plant profile

Plant Name: _____

Botanical Name: _____

Supplier: _____

annual ◯   biennial ◯   perennial ◯

Location: _____

Fertilizer/Soil: _____

Pest/Weed Control: _____

flower ◯   herb ◯   fruit ◯   vegetable ◯   shrub ◯   tree ◯

Bloom/Harvest: _____

Pruning: _____

Transplant/Propagate/Divide: _____

Full ◯   Partial ◯   Shade ◯

Size at maturity: _____

_____

plant notes

....

....

....

....

....

....

....

....

....

....

....

....

plant profile

Plant Name: _____

Botanical Name: _____

Supplier: _____

annual ⬭   biennial ⬭   perennial ⬭

Location: _____

Fertilizer/Soil: _____

Pest/Weed Control: _____

flower ⬭   herb ⬭   fruit ⬭   vegetable ⬭   shrub ⬭   tree ⬭

Bloom/Harvest: _____

Pruning: _____

Transplant/Propagate/Divide: _____

Full ⬭   Partial ⬭   Shade ⬭

Size at maturity: _____

_____

plant notes

....

....

....

....

....

....

....

....

....

....

....

....

plant profile

Plant Name:

Botanical Name:

Supplier:

annual ⬭ biennial ⬭ perennial ⬭

Location:

Fertilizer/Soil:

Pest/Weed Control:

flower ⬭ herb ⬭ fruit ⬭ vegetable ⬭ shrub ⬭ tree ⬭

Bloom/Harvest:

Pruning:

Transplant/Propagate/Divide:

Full ⬭ Partial ⬭ Shade ⬭

Size at maturity:

plant notes

....

....

....

....

....

....

....

....

....

....

....

....

plant profile

Plant Name:

Botanical Name:

Supplier:

annual ⬛   biennial ⬛   perennial ⬛

Location:

Fertilizer/Soil:

Pest/Weed Control:

flower⬛   herb⬛   fruit⬛   vegetable⬛   shrub⬛   tree⬛

Bloom/Harvest:

Pruning:

Transplant/Propagate/Divide:

Full⬛   Partial⬛   Shade⬛

Size at maturity:

plant notes

....

....

....

....

....

....

....

....

....

....

....

....

plant profile

Plant Name: _____

Botanical Name: _____

Supplier: _____

annual ⬜   biennial ⬜   perennial ⬜

Location: _____

Fertilizer/Soil: _____

Pest/Weed Control: _____

flower ⬜   herb ⬜   fruit ⬜   vegetable ⬜   shrub ⬜   tree ⬜

Bloom/Harvest: _____

Pruning: _____

Transplant/Propagate/Divide: _____

Full ⬜   Partial ⬜   Shade ⬜

Size at maturity: _____

_____

plant notes

....

....

....

....

....

....

....

....

....

....

....

....

plant profile

Plant Name:

_____

Botanical Name:

_____

Supplier:

_____

annual ⬭   biennial ⬭   perennial ⬭

Location: _____

Fertilizer/Soil: _____

Pest/Weed Control: _____

flower ⬭   herb ⬭   fruit ⬭   vegetable ⬭   shrub ⬭   tree ⬭

Bloom/Harvest:

_____

Pruning:

_____

Transplant/Propagate/Divide: _____

Full ⬭   Partial ⬭   Shade ⬭

Size at maturity:

_____

_____

plant notes

....

....

....

....

....

....

....

....

....

....

....

....

plant profile

Plant Name:

_____

Botanical Name:

_____

Supplier:

_____

annual ☐   biennial ☐   perennial ☐

Location: _____

Fertilizer/Soil: _____

Pest/Weed Control: _____

flower ☐   herb ☐   fruit ☐   vegetable ☐   shrub ☐   tree ☐

Bloom/Harvest: _____

Pruning: _____

Transplant/Propagate/Divide: _____

Full ☐   Partial ☐   Shade ☐

Size at maturity:

_____

_____

plant notes

....

....

....

....

....

....

....

....

....

....

....

....

plant profile

Plant Name:
_____

Botanical Name:
_____

Supplier:
_____

annual ◯   biennial ◯   perennial ◯

Location: _____

Fertilizer/Soil: _____

Pest/Weed Control: _____

flower ◯   herb ◯   fruit ◯   vegetable ◯   shrub ◯   tree ◯

Bloom/Harvest: _____

Pruning: _____

Transplant/Propagate/Divide: _____

Full ◯   Partial ◯   Shade ◯

Size at maturity:
_____

_____

plant notes

....

....

....

....

....

....

....

....

....

....

....

....

plant profile

Plant Name:
_____

Botanical Name:
_____

Supplier:
_____

annual ◯　　biennial ◯　　perennial ◯

Location: _____

Fertilizer/Soil: _____

Pest/Weed Control: _____

flower ◯　herb ◯　fruit ◯　vegetable ◯　shrub ◯　tree ◯

Bloom/Harvest: _____

Pruning: _____

Transplant/Propagate/Divide: _____

Full ◯　Partial ◯　Shade ◯

Size at maturity:
_____

_____

plant notes

....

....

....

....

....

....

....

....

....

....

....

....

plant profile

Plant Name:
_____

Botanical Name:
_____

Supplier:
_____

annual ⬜   biennial ⬜   perennial ⬜

Location: _____

Fertilizer/Soil: _____

Pest/Weed Control: _____

flower ⬜   herb ⬜   fruit ⬜   vegetable ⬜   shrub ⬜   tree ⬜

Bloom/Harvest:
_____

Pruning:
_____

Transplant/Propagate/Divide: _____

Full ⬜   Partial ⬜   Shade ⬜

Size at maturity:
_____

_____

plant notes

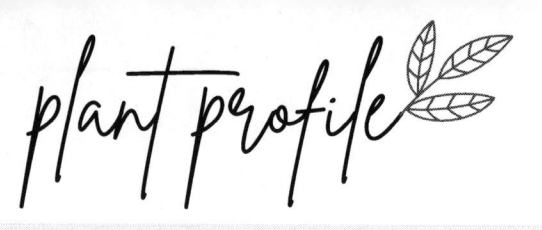

plant profile

Plant Name: _____

Botanical Name: _____

Supplier: _____

annual ⬭　biennial ⬭　perennial ⬭

Location: _____

Fertilizer/Soil: _____

Pest/Weed Control: _____

flower ⬭　herb ⬭　fruit ⬭　vegetable ⬭　shrub ⬭　tree ⬭

Bloom/Harvest: _____

Pruning: _____

Transplant/Propagate/Divide: _____

Full ⬭　Partial ⬭　Shade ⬭

Size at maturity: _____

_____

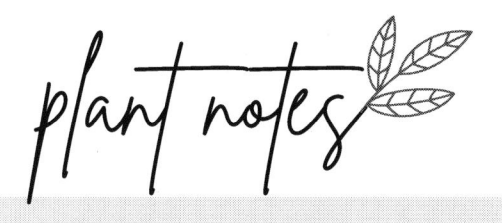

plant notes

....

....

....

....

....

....

....

....

....

....

....

....

plant profile

Plant Name:

Botanical Name:

Supplier:

annual 〇   biennial 〇   perennial 〇

Location:

Fertilizer/Soil:

Pest/Weed Control:

flower 〇   herb 〇   fruit 〇   vegetable 〇   shrub 〇   tree 〇

Bloom/Harvest:

Pruning:

Transplant/Propagate/Divide:

Full 〇   Partial 〇   Shade 〇

Size at maturity:

....

....

....

....

....

....

....

....

....

....

....

plant profile

Plant Name: _____

Botanical Name: _____

Supplier: _____

annual ⬭ biennial ⬭ perennial ⬭

Location: _____

Fertilizer/Soil: _____

Pest/Weed Control: _____

flower ⬭ herb ⬭ fruit ⬭ vegetable ⬭ shrub ⬭ tree ⬭

Bloom/Harvest: _____

Pruning: _____

Transplant/Propagate/Divide: _____

Full ⬭ Partial ⬭ Shade ⬭

Size at maturity: _____

_____

plant notes

plant profile

Plant Name: _____

Botanical Name: _____

Supplier: _____

annual ⭕   biennial ⭕   perennial ⭕

Location: _____

Fertilizer/Soil: _____

Pest/Weed Control: _____

flower ⭕   herb ⭕   fruit ⭕   vegetable ⭕   shrub ⭕   tree ⭕

Bloom/Harvest: _____

Pruning: _____

Transplant/Propagate/Divide: _____

Full ⭕   Partial ⭕   Shade ⭕

Size at maturity: _____

_____

plant notes

plant profile

Plant Name: _____

Botanical Name: _____

Supplier: _____

annual ⬭   biennial ⬭   perennial ⬭

Location: _____

Fertilizer/Soil: _____

Pest/Weed Control: _____

flower⬭   herb⬭   fruit⬭   vegetable⬭   shrub⬭   tree⬭

Bloom/Harvest: _____

Pruning: _____

Transplant/Propagate/Divide: _____

Full⬭   Partial⬭   Shade⬭

Size at maturity: _____

_____

plant notes

....

....

....

....

....

....

....

....

....

....

....

....

plant profile

Plant Name: _____

Botanical Name: _____

Supplier: _____

annual ⭕   biennial ⭕   perennial ⭕

Location: _____

Fertilizer/Soil: _____

Pest/Weed Control: _____

flower ⭕   herb ⭕   fruit ⭕   vegetable ⭕   shrub ⭕   tree ⭕

Bloom/Harvest: _____

Pruning: _____

Transplant/Propagate/Divide: _____

Full ⭕   Partial ⭕   Shade ⭕

Size at maturity: _____

_____

plant notes

plant profile

Plant Name:

Botanical Name:

Supplier:

annual ⬭   biennial ⬭   perennial ⬭

Location:

Fertilizer/Soil:

Pest/Weed Control:

flower ⬭   herb ⬭   fruit ⬭   vegetable ⬭   shrub ⬭   tree ⬭

Bloom/Harvest:

Pruning:

Transplant/Propagate/Divide:

Full ⬭   Partial ⬭   Shade ⬭

Size at maturity:

plant notes

....

....

....

....

....

....

....

....

....

....

....

....

plant profile

Plant Name: _____

Botanical Name: _____

Supplier: _____

annual ⬭   biennial ⬭   perennial ⬭

Location: _____

Fertilizer/Soil: _____

Pest/Weed Control: _____

flower ⬭   herb ⬭   fruit ⬭   vegetable ⬭   shrub ⬭   tree ⬭

Bloom/Harvest: _____

Pruning: _____

Transplant/Propagate/Divide: _____

Full ⬭   Partial ⬭   Shade ⬭

Size at maturity: _____

_____

....

....

....

....

....

....

....

....

....

....

....

....

plant profile

Plant Name:

Botanical Name:

Supplier:

annual ⬜   biennial ⬜   perennial ⬜

Location:

Fertilizer/Soil:

Pest/Weed Control:

flower ⬜   herb ⬜   fruit ⬜   vegetable ⬜   shrub ⬜   tree ⬜

Bloom/Harvest:

Pruning:

Transplant/Propagate/Divide:

Full ⬜   Partial ⬜   Shade ⬜

Size at maturity:

plant notes

plant profile

Plant Name:

Botanical Name:

Supplier:

annual ⬭ biennial ⬭ perennial ⬭

Location:

Fertilizer/Soil:

Pest/Weed Control:

flower ⬭ herb ⬭ fruit ⬭ vegetable ⬭ shrub ⬭ tree ⬭

Bloom/Harvest:

Pruning:

Transplant/Propagate/Divide:

Full ⬭ Partial ⬭ Shade ⬭

Size at maturity:

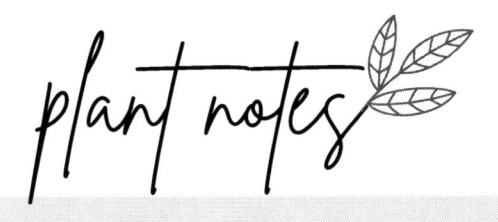

plant notes

....

....

....

....

....

....

....

....

....

....

....

....

plant profile

Plant Name: _____

Botanical Name: _____

Supplier: _____

annual ⭕ biennial ⭕ perennial ⭕

Location: _____

Fertilizer/Soil: _____

Pest/Weed Control: _____

flower⭕ herb⭕ fruit⭕ vegetable⭕ shrub⭕ tree⭕

Bloom/Harvest: _____

Pruning: _____

Transplant/Propagate/Divide: _____

Full⭕ Partial⭕ Shade⭕

Size at maturity: _____

_____

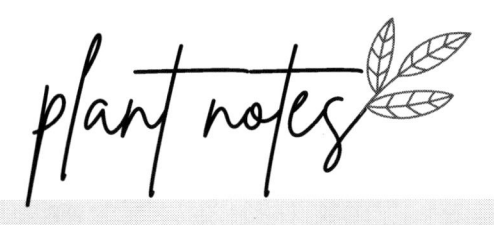

plant notes

....

....

....

....

....

....

....

....

....

....

....

....

plant profile

Plant Name:
_____

Botanical Name:
_____

Supplier:
_____

annual ⬜   biennial ⬜   perennial ⬜

Location: _____

Fertilizer/Soil: _____

Pest/Weed Control: _____

flower ⬜   herb ⬜   fruit ⬜   vegetable ⬜   shrub ⬜   tree ⬜

Bloom/Harvest: _____

Pruning: _____

Transplant/Propagate/Divide: _____

Full ⬜   Partial ⬜   Shade ⬜

Size at maturity:
_____

_____

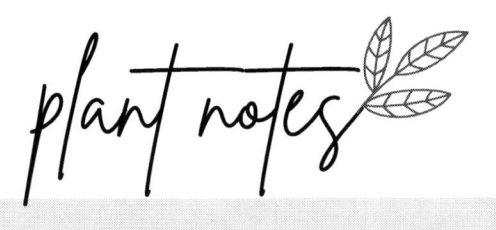

plant notes

....

....

....

....

....

....

....

....

....

....

....

....

....

plant profile

Plant Name:

_____

Botanical Name:

_____

Supplier:

_____

annual ⬜   biennial ⬜   perennial ⬜

Location: _____

Fertilizer/Soil: _____

Pest/Weed Control: _____

flower ⬜   herb ⬜   fruit ⬜   vegetable ⬜   shrub ⬜   tree ⬜

Bloom/Harvest: _____

Pruning: _____

Transplant/Propagate/Divide: _____

Full ⬜   Partial ⬜   Shade ⬜

Size at maturity:

_____

_____

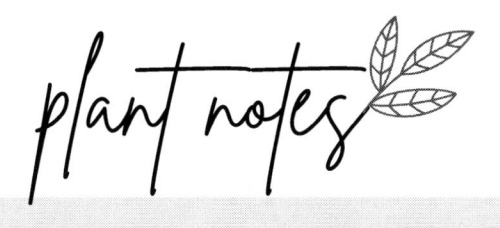

plant notes

....

....

....

....

....

....

....

....

....

....

....

....

plant profile

Plant Name:

Botanical Name:

Supplier:

annual ⬭   biennial ⬭   perennial ⬭

Location:

Fertilizer/Soil:

Pest/Weed Control:

flower ⬭   herb ⬭   fruit ⬭   vegetable ⬭   shrub ⬭   tree ⬭

Bloom/Harvest:

Pruning:

Transplant/Propagate/Divide:

Full ⬭   Partial ⬭   Shade ⬭

Size at maturity:

plant notes

....

....

....

....

....

....

....

....

....

....

....

....

plant profile

Plant Name:

Botanical Name:

Supplier:

annual ◯   biennial ◯   perennial ◯

Location:

Fertilizer/Soil:

Pest/Weed Control:

flower ◯   herb ◯   fruit ◯   vegetable ◯   shrub ◯   tree ◯

Bloom/Harvest:

Pruning:

Transplant/Propagate/Divide:

Full ◯   Partial ◯   Shade ◯

Size at maturity:

plant notes

··

··

··

··

··

··

··

··

··

··

··

··

plant profile

Plant Name:
_____

Botanical Name:
_____

Supplier:
_____

annual ⬜   biennial ⬜   perennial ⬜

Location: _____

Fertilizer/Soil: _____

Pest/Weed Control: _____

flower ⬜   herb ⬜   fruit ⬜   vegetable ⬜   shrub ⬜   tree ⬜

Bloom/Harvest: _____

Pruning: _____

Transplant/Propagate/Divide: _____

Full ⬜   Partial ⬜   Shade ⬜

Size at maturity:
_____

_____

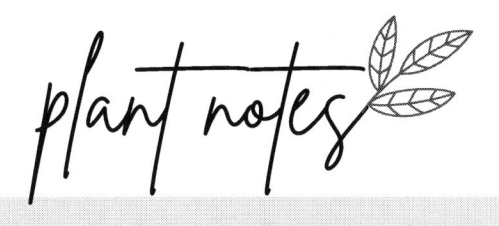

plant notes

···

···

···

···

···

···

···

···

···

···

···

···

plant profile

Plant Name:
_____

Botanical Name:
_____

Supplier:
_____

annual ☐   biennial ☐   perennial ☐

Location: _____

Fertilizer/Soil: _____

Pest/Weed Control: _____

flower ☐   herb ☐   fruit ☐   vegetable ☐   shrub ☐   tree ☐

Bloom/Harvest: _____

Pruning: _____

Transplant/Propagate/Divide: _____

Full ☐   Partial ☐   Shade ☐

Size at maturity:
_____

_____

plant notes

plant profile

Plant Name:

Botanical Name:

Supplier:

annual ⬭   biennial ⬭   perennial ⬭

Location:

Fertilizer/Soil:

Pest/Weed Control:

flower ⬭   herb ⬭   fruit ⬭   vegetable ⬭   shrub ⬭   tree ⬭

Bloom/Harvest:

Pruning:

Transplant/Propagate/Divide:

Full ⬭   Partial ⬭   Shade ⬭

Size at maturity:

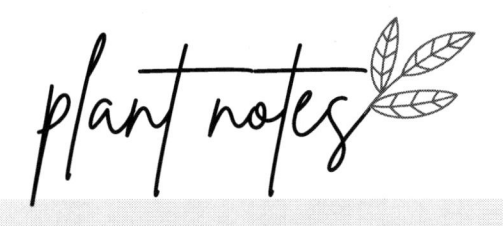

plant notes

··

··

··

··

··

··

··

··

··

··

··

plant profile

Plant Name: _____

Botanical Name: _____

Supplier: _____

annual ⬜   biennial ⬜   perennial ⬜

Location: _____

Fertilizer/Soil: _____

Pest/Weed Control: _____

flower ⬜   herb ⬜   fruit ⬜   vegetable ⬜   shrub ⬜   tree ⬜

Bloom/Harvest: _____

Pruning: _____

Transplant/Propagate/Divide: _____

Full ⬜   Partial ⬜   Shade ⬜

Size at maturity: _____

_____

plant notes

....

....

....

....

....

....

....

....

....

....

....

....

plant profile

Plant Name:
_____

Botanical Name:
_____

Supplier:
_____

annual ☐   biennial ☐   perennial ☐

Location: _____

Fertilizer/Soil: _____

Pest/Weed Control: _____

flower ☐   herb ☐   fruit ☐   vegetable ☐   shrub ☐   tree ☐

Bloom/Harvest: _____

Pruning: _____

Transplant/Propagate/Divide: _____

Full ☐   Partial ☐   Shade ☐

Size at maturity:
_____

_____

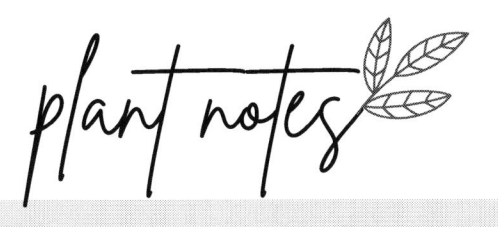

plant notes

....

....

....

....

....

....

....

....

....

....

....

....

plant profile

Plant Name:

Botanical Name:

Supplier:

annual ⭘   biennial ⭘   perennial ⭘

Location:

Fertilizer/Soil:

Pest/Weed Control:

flower ⭘   herb ⭘   fruit ⭘   vegetable ⭘   shrub ⭘   tree ⭘

Bloom/Harvest:

Pruning:

Transplant/Propagate/Divide:

Full ⭘   Partial ⭘   Shade ⭘

Size at maturity:

plant notes

....

....

....

....

....

....

....

....

....

....

....

plant profile

Plant Name:

Botanical Name:

Supplier:

annual ⬭ biennial ⬭ perennial ⬭

Location:

Fertilizer/Soil:

Pest/Weed Control:

flower⬭ herb⬭ fruit⬭ vegetable⬭ shrub⬭ tree⬭

Bloom/Harvest:

Pruning:

Transplant/Propagate/Divide:

Full⬭ Partial⬭ Shade⬭

Size at maturity:

plant notes

plant profile

Plant Name:

_____

Botanical Name:

_____

Supplier:

_____

annual ⭘   biennial ⭘   perennial ⭘

Location: _____

Fertilizer/Soil: _____

Pest/Weed Control: _____

flower ⭘   herb ⭘   fruit ⭘   vegetable ⭘   shrub ⭘   tree ⭘

Bloom/Harvest:

_____

Pruning: _____

Transplant/Propagate/Divide: _____

Full ⭘   Partial ⭘   Shade ⭘

Size at maturity:

_____

_____

plant notes

....

....

....

....

....

....

....

....

....

....

....

....

plant profile

Plant Name: _____

Botanical Name: _____

Supplier: _____

annual ⬜   biennial ⬜   perennial ⬜

Location: _____

Fertilizer/Soil: _____

Pest/Weed Control: _____

flower ⬜   herb ⬜   fruit ⬜   vegetable ⬜   shrub ⬜   tree ⬜

Bloom/Harvest: _____

Pruning: _____

Transplant/Propagate/Divide: _____

Full ⬜   Partial ⬜   Shade ⬜

Size at maturity: _____

_____

plant profile

Plant Name:

Botanical Name:

Supplier:

annual ◯   biennial ◯   perennial ◯

Location:

Fertilizer/Soil:

Pest/Weed Control:

flower ◯   herb ◯   fruit ◯   vegetable ◯   shrub ◯   tree ◯

Bloom/Harvest:

Pruning:

Transplant/Propagate/Divide:

Full ◯   Partial ◯   Shade ◯

Size at maturity:

plant profile

Plant Name: _____

Botanical Name: _____

Supplier: _____

annual ⬭   biennial ⬭   perennial ⬭

Location: _____

Fertilizer/Soil: _____

Pest/Weed Control: _____

flower ⬭   herb ⬭   fruit ⬭   vegetable ⬭   shrub ⬭   tree ⬭

Bloom/Harvest: _____

Pruning: _____

Transplant/Propagate/Divide: _____

Full ⬭   Partial ⬭   Shade ⬭

Size at maturity: _____

_____

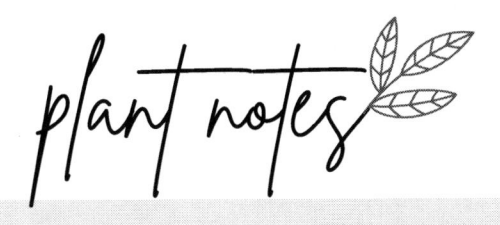

plant notes

plant profile

Plant Name: _____

Botanical Name: _____

Supplier: _____

annual ⬚ biennial ⬚ perennial ⬚

Location: _____

Fertilizer/Soil: _____

Pest/Weed Control: _____

flower ⬚ herb ⬚ fruit ⬚ vegetable ⬚ shrub ⬚ tree ⬚

Bloom/Harvest: _____

Pruning: _____

Transplant/Propagate/Divide: _____

Full ⬚ Partial ⬚ Shade ⬚

Size at maturity: _____

_____

plant profile

Plant Name:

_____

Botanical Name:

_____

Supplier:

_____

annual ⬭ biennial ⬭ perennial ⬭

Location: _____

Fertilizer/Soil: _____

Pest/Weed Control: _____

flower ⬭ herb ⬭ fruit ⬭ vegetable ⬭ shrub ⬭ tree ⬭

Bloom/Harvest: _____

Pruning: _____

Transplant/Propagate/Divide: _____

Full ⬭ Partial ⬭ Shade ⬭

Size at maturity:

_____

_____

plant profile

Plant Name:

Botanical Name:

Supplier:

annual ⬜   biennial ⬜   perennial ⬜

Location:

Fertilizer/Soil:

Pest/Weed Control:

flower ⬜   herb ⬜   fruit ⬜   vegetable ⬜   shrub ⬜   tree ⬜

Bloom/Harvest:

Pruning:

Transplant/Propagate/Divide:

Full ⬜   Partial ⬜   Shade ⬜

Size at maturity:

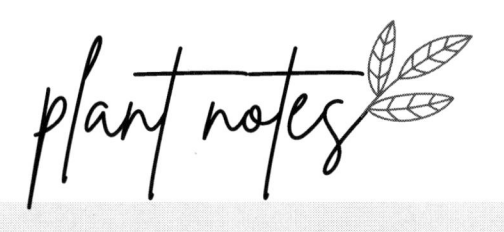

plant notes

....

....

....

....

....

....

....

....

....

....

....

....

plant profile

Plant Name: _____

Botanical Name: _____

Supplier: _____

annual ⬭ biennial ⬭ perennial ⬭

Location: _____

Fertilizer/Soil: _____

Pest/Weed Control: _____

flower ⬭ herb ⬭ fruit ⬭ vegetable ⬭ shrub ⬭ tree ⬭

Bloom/Harvest: _____

Pruning: _____

Transplant/Propagate/Divide: _____

Full ⬭ Partial ⬭ Shade ⬭

Size at maturity: _____

_____

plant notes

....

....

....

....

....

....

....

....

....

....

....

....

plant profile

Plant Name: _____

Botanical Name: _____

Supplier: _____

annual ☐   biennial ☐   perennial ☐

Location: _____

Fertilizer/Soil: _____

Pest/Weed Control: _____

flower ☐   herb ☐   fruit ☐   vegetable ☐   shrub ☐   tree ☐

Bloom/Harvest: _____

Pruning: _____

Transplant/Propagate/Divide: _____

Full ☐   Partial ☐   Shade ☐

Size at maturity: _____

_____

plant notes

....

....

....

....

....

....

....

....

....

....

....

....

plant profile

Plant Name:
_____

Botanical Name:
_____

Supplier:
_____

annual ⬜   biennial ⬜   perennial ⬜

Location: _____

Fertilizer/Soil: _____

Pest/Weed Control: _____

flower ⬜   herb ⬜   fruit ⬜   vegetable ⬜   shrub ⬜   tree ⬜

Bloom/Harvest: _____

Pruning: _____

Transplant/Propagate/Divide: _____

Full ⬜   Partial ⬜   Shade ⬜

Size at maturity:
_____

_____

plant notes

....

....

....

....

....

....

....

....

....

....

....

....

plant profile

Plant Name:

Botanical Name:

Supplier:

annual ⬚ biennial ⬚ perennial ⬚

Location:

Fertilizer/Soil:

Pest/Weed Control:

flower ⬚ herb ⬚ fruit ⬚ vegetable ⬚ shrub ⬚ tree ⬚

Bloom/Harvest:

Pruning:

Transplant/Propagate/Divide:

Full ⬚ Partial ⬚ Shade ⬚

Size at maturity:

plant notes

....

....

....

....

....

....

....

....

....

....

....

....

plant profile

Plant Name:
_____

Botanical Name:
_____

Supplier:
_____

annual ◯   biennial ◯   perennial ◯

Location: _____

Fertilizer/Soil: _____

Pest/Weed Control: _____

flower ◯   herb ◯   fruit ◯   vegetable ◯   shrub ◯   tree ◯

Bloom/Harvest: _____

Pruning: _____

Transplant/Propagate/Divide: _____

Full ◯   Partial ◯   Shade ◯

Size at maturity:
_____

_____

plant notes

....

....

....

....

....

....

....

....

....

....

....

....

plant profile

Plant Name:
_____

Botanical Name:
_____

Supplier:
_____

annual ◯   biennial ◯   perennial ◯

Location: _____

Fertilizer/Soil: _____

Pest/Weed Control: _____

flower ◯   herb ◯   fruit ◯   vegetable ◯   shrub ◯   tree ◯

Bloom/Harvest:
_____

Pruning: _____

Transplant/Propagate/Divide: _____

☀ Full ◯   Partial ◯   Shade ◯

Size at maturity:
_____

_____

plant notes

plant profile

Plant Name: _____

Botanical Name: _____

Supplier: _____

annual ⭕   biennial ⭕   perennial ⭕

Location: _____

Fertilizer/Soil: _____

Pest/Weed Control: _____

flower ⭕   herb ⭕   fruit ⭕   vegetable ⭕   shrub ⭕   tree ⭕

Bloom/Harvest: _____

Pruning: _____

Transplant/Propagate/Divide: _____

Full ⭕   Partial ⭕   Shade ⭕

Size at maturity: _____

_____

plant notes

....

....

....

....

....

....

....

....

....

....

....

....

plant profile

Plant Name:

Botanical Name:

Supplier:

annual ⬚   biennial ⬚   perennial ⬚

Location:

Fertilizer/Soil:

Pest/Weed Control:

flower ⬚   herb ⬚   fruit ⬚   vegetable ⬚   shrub ⬚   tree ⬚

Bloom/Harvest:

Pruning:

Transplant/Propagate/Divide:

Full ⬚   Partial ⬚   Shade ⬚

Size at maturity:

plant notes

....

....

....

....

....

....

....

....

....

....

....

....

plant profile

Plant Name: _____

Botanical Name: _____

Supplier: _____

annual ⬜   biennial ⬜   perennial ⬜

Location: _____

Fertilizer/Soil: _____

Pest/Weed Control: _____

flower ⬜   herb ⬜   fruit ⬜   vegetable ⬜   shrub ⬜   tree ⬜

Bloom/Harvest: _____

Pruning: _____

Transplant/Propagate/Divide: _____

Full ⬜   Partial ⬜   Shade ⬜

Size at maturity: _____

_____

plant notes

plant profile

Plant Name: _____

Botanical Name: _____

Supplier: _____

annual ⭕ biennial ⭕ perennial ⭕

Location: _____

Fertilizer/Soil: _____

Pest/Weed Control: _____

flower⭕ herb⭕ fruit⭕ vegetable⭕ shrub⭕ tree⭕

Bloom/Harvest: _____

Pruning: _____

Transplant/Propagate/Divide: _____

Full⭕ Partial⭕ Shade⭕

Size at maturity: _____

_____

plant notes

....

....

....

....

....

....

....

....

....

....

....

....

plant profile

Plant Name:

Botanical Name:

Supplier:

annual ⬜   biennial ⬜   perennial ⬜

Location:

Fertilizer/Soil:

Pest/Weed Control:

flower ⬜   herb ⬜   fruit ⬜   vegetable ⬜   shrub ⬜   tree ⬜

Bloom/Harvest:

Pruning:

Transplant/Propagate/Divide:

Full ⬜   Partial ⬜   Shade ⬜

Size at maturity:

plant notes

plant profile

Plant Name:

_____

Botanical Name:

_____

Supplier:

_____

annual ○   biennial ○   perennial ○

Location: _____

Fertilizer/Soil: _____

Pest/Weed Control: _____

flower ○   herb ○   fruit ○   vegetable ○   shrub ○   tree ○

Bloom/Harvest: _____

Pruning: _____

Transplant/Propagate/Divide: _____

Full ○   Partial ○   Shade ○

Size at maturity:

_____

_____

plant notes

plant profile

Plant Name: _____

Botanical Name: _____

Supplier: _____

annual ☐   biennial ☐   perennial ☐

Location: _____

Fertilizer/Soil: _____

Pest/Weed Control: _____

flower ☐   herb ☐   fruit ☐   vegetable ☐   shrub ☐   tree ☐

Bloom/Harvest: _____

Pruning: _____

Transplant/Propagate/Divide: _____

Full ☐   Partial ☐   Shade ☐

Size at maturity: _____

_____

plant notes

....

....

....

....

....

....

....

....

....

....

....

....

plant profile

Plant Name:

Botanical Name:

Supplier:

annual ⬭   biennial ⬭   perennial ⬭

Location:

Fertilizer/Soil:

Pest/Weed Control:

flower⬭   herb⬭   fruit⬭   vegetable⬭   shrub⬭   tree⬭

Bloom/Harvest:

Pruning:

Transplant/Propagate/Divide:

Full⬭   Partial⬭   Shade⬭

Size at maturity:

plant notes

....

....

....

....

....

....

....

....

....

....

....

....

plant profile

Plant Name: _____

Botanical Name: _____

Supplier: _____

annual ⬜   biennial ⬜   perennial ⬜

Location: _____

Fertilizer/Soil: _____

Pest/Weed Control: _____

flower ⬜   herb ⬜   fruit ⬜   vegetable ⬜   shrub ⬜   tree ⬜

Bloom/Harvest: _____

Pruning: _____

Transplant/Propagate/Divide: _____

Full ⬜   Partial ⬜   Shade ⬜

Size at maturity: _____

_____

plant notes

....

....

....

....

....

....

....

....

....

....

....

plant profile

Plant Name:
_____

Botanical Name:
_____

Supplier:
_____

annual ⬜ biennial ⬜ perennial ⬜

Location: _____

Fertilizer/Soil: _____

Pest/Weed Control: _____

flower⬜ herb⬜ fruit⬜ vegetable⬜ shrub⬜ tree⬜

Bloom/Harvest: _____

Pruning: _____

Transplant/Propagate/Divide: _____

Full⬜ Partial⬜ Shade⬜

Size at maturity:
_____

_____

plant profile

Plant Name:

Botanical Name:

Supplier:

annual ⭕   biennial ⭕   perennial ⭕

Location:

Fertilizer/Soil:

Pest/Weed Control:

flower ⭕   herb ⭕   fruit ⭕   vegetable ⭕   shrub ⭕   tree ⭕

Bloom/Harvest:

Pruning:

Transplant/Propagate/Divide:

Full ⭕   Partial ⭕   Shade ⭕

Size at maturity:

....

....

....

....

....

....

....

....

....

....

....

....

plant profile

Plant Name:

Botanical Name:

Supplier:

annual ⬭   biennial ⬭   perennial ⬭

Location:

Fertilizer/Soil:

Pest/Weed Control:

flower ⬭   herb ⬭   fruit ⬭   vegetable ⬭   shrub ⬭   tree ⬭

Bloom/Harvest:

Pruning:

Transplant/Propagate/Divide:

Full ⬭   Partial ⬭   Shade ⬭

Size at maturity:

plant notes

·······································

·······································

·······································

·······································

·······································

·······································

·······································

·······································

·······································

·······································

·······································

·······································

plant profile

Plant Name:

Botanical Name:

Supplier:

annual ⬜   biennial ⬜   perennial ⬜

Location:

Fertilizer/Soil:

Pest/Weed Control:

flower ⬜   herb ⬜   fruit ⬜   vegetable ⬜   shrub ⬜   tree ⬜

Bloom/Harvest:

Pruning:

Transplant/Propagate/Divide:

Full ⬜   Partial ⬜   Shade ⬜

Size at maturity:

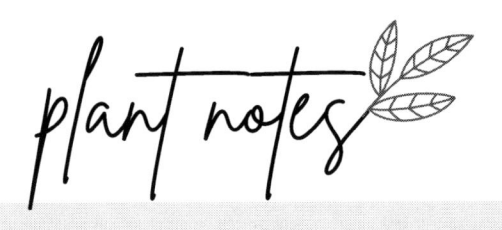

plant notes

....

....

....

....

....

....

....

....

....

....

....

....

plant profile

Plant Name: _____

Botanical Name: _____

Supplier: _____

annual ☐   biennial ☐   perennial ☐

Location: _____

Fertilizer/Soil: _____

Pest/Weed Control: _____

flower ☐   herb ☐   fruit ☐   vegetable ☐   shrub ☐   tree ☐

Bloom/Harvest: _____

Pruning: _____

Transplant/Propagate/Divide: _____

Full ☐   Partial ☐   Shade ☐

Size at maturity: _____

_____

plant notes

....

....

....

....

....

....

....

....

....

....

....

....

plant profile

Plant Name:
_____

Botanical Name:
_____

Supplier:
_____

annual ⬛   biennial ⬛   perennial ⬛

Location: _____

Fertilizer/Soil: _____

Pest/Weed Control: _____

flower ⬛   herb ⬛   fruit ⬛   vegetable ⬛   shrub ⬛   tree ⬛

Bloom/Harvest: _____

Pruning: _____

Transplant/Propagate/Divide: _____

Full ⬛   Partial ⬛   Shade ⬛

Size at maturity:
_____

_____

plant notes

....

....

....

....

....

....

....

....

....

....

....

....

plant profile

Plant Name: _____

Botanical Name: _____

Supplier: _____

annual ⬜ biennial ⬜ perennial ⬜

Location: _____

Fertilizer/Soil: _____

Pest/Weed Control: _____

flower⬜ herb⬜ fruit⬜ vegetable⬜ shrub⬜ tree⬜

Bloom/Harvest: _____

Pruning: _____

Transplant/Propagate/Divide: _____

Full⬜ Partial⬜ Shade⬜

Size at maturity: _____

_____

plant notes

plant profile

Plant Name:

Botanical Name:

Supplier:

annual ☐   biennial ☐   perennial ☐

Location:

Fertilizer/Soil:

Pest/Weed Control:

flower ☐   herb ☐   fruit ☐   vegetable ☐   shrub ☐   tree ☐

Bloom/Harvest:

Pruning:

Transplant/Propagate/Divide:

Full ☐   Partial ☐   Shade ☐

Size at maturity:

plant notes

....

....

....

....

....

....

....

....

....

....

....

....

plant profile

Plant Name: _____

Botanical Name: _____

Supplier: _____

annual ⬜ biennial ⬜ perennial ⬜

Location: _____

Fertilizer/Soil: _____

Pest/Weed Control: _____

flower ⬜ herb ⬜ fruit ⬜ vegetable ⬜ shrub ⬜ tree ⬜

Bloom/Harvest: _____

Pruning: _____

Transplant/Propagate/Divide: _____

Full ⬜ Partial ⬜ Shade ⬜

Size at maturity: _____

_____

plant notes

plant profile

Plant Name:

Botanical Name:

Supplier:

annual ⬜   biennial ⬜   perennial ⬜

Location:

Fertilizer/Soil:

Pest/Weed Control:

flower⬜   herb⬜   fruit⬜   vegetable⬜   shrub⬜   tree⬜

Bloom/Harvest:

Pruning:

Transplant/Propagate/Divide:

Full⬜   Partial⬜   Shade⬜

Size at maturity:

....

....

....

....

....

....

....

....

....

....

....

....

plant profile

Plant Name: _____

Botanical Name: _____

Supplier: _____

annual ☐   biennial ☐   perennial ☐

Location: _____

Fertilizer/Soil: _____

Pest/Weed Control: _____

flower ☐   herb ☐   fruit ☐   vegetable ☐   shrub ☐   tree ☐

Bloom/Harvest: _____

Pruning: _____

Transplant/Propagate/Divide: _____

Full ☐   Partial ☐   Shade ☐

Size at maturity: _____

_____

plant notes

··

··

··

··

··

··

··

··

··

··

··

··

plant profile

Plant Name: _____

Botanical Name: _____

Supplier: _____

annual ⬜   biennial ⬜   perennial ⬜

Location: _____

Fertilizer/Soil: _____

Pest/Weed Control: _____

flower ⬜   herb ⬜   fruit ⬜   vegetable ⬜   shrub ⬜   tree ⬜

Bloom/Harvest: _____

Pruning: _____

Transplant/Propagate/Divide: _____

Full ⬜   Partial ⬜   Shade ⬜

Size at maturity: _____

_____

plant notes

....

....

....

....

....

....

....

....

....

....

....

....

plant profile

Plant Name: _____

Botanical Name: _____

Supplier: _____

annual ⬜   biennial ⬜   perennial ⬜

Location: _____

Fertilizer/Soil: _____

Pest/Weed Control: _____

flower ⬜   herb ⬜   fruit ⬜   vegetable ⬜   shrub ⬜   tree ⬜

Bloom/Harvest: _____

Pruning: _____

Transplant/Propagate/Divide: _____

Full ⬜   Partial ⬜   Shade ⬜

Size at maturity: _____

_____

plant notes

....

....

....

....

....

....

....

....

....

....

....

....

plant profile

Plant Name: _____

Botanical Name: _____

Supplier: _____

annual ☐   biennial ☐   perennial ☐

Location: _____

Fertilizer/Soil: _____

Pest/Weed Control: _____

flower ☐   herb ☐   fruit ☐   vegetable ☐   shrub ☐   tree ☐

Bloom/Harvest: _____

Pruning: _____

Transplant/Propagate/Divide: _____

Full ☐   Partial ☐   Shade ☐

Size at maturity: _____

_____

plant notes

....

....

....

....

....

....

....

....

....

....

....

....

plant profile

Plant Name: _____

Botanical Name: _____

Supplier: _____

annual ⭕ biennial ⭕ perennial ⭕

Location: _____

Fertilizer/Soil: _____

Pest/Weed Control: _____

flower ⭕ herb ⭕ fruit ⭕ vegetable ⭕ shrub ⭕ tree ⭕

Bloom/Harvest: _____

Pruning: _____

Transplant/Propagate/Divide: _____

Full ⭕ Partial ⭕ Shade ⭕

Size at maturity: _____

_____

plant profile

Plant Name:

Botanical Name:

Supplier:

annual ⬭   biennial ⬭   perennial ⬭

Location:

Fertilizer/Soil:

Pest/Weed Control:

flower ⬭ herb ⬭ fruit ⬭ vegetable ⬭ shrub ⬭ tree ⬭

Bloom/Harvest:

Pruning:

Transplant/Propagate/Divide:

Full ⬭ Partial ⬭ Shade ⬭

Size at maturity:

plant notes

plant profile

Plant Name: _____

Botanical Name: _____

Supplier: _____

annual ⬚   biennial ⬚   perennial ⬚

Location: _____

Fertilizer/Soil: _____

Pest/Weed Control: _____

flower ⬚   herb ⬚   fruit ⬚   vegetable ⬚   shrub ⬚   tree ⬚

Bloom/Harvest: _____

Pruning: _____

Transplant/Propagate/Divide: _____

Full ⬚   Partial ⬚   Shade ⬚

Size at maturity: _____

_____

plant notes

....

....

....

....

....

....

....

....

....

....

....

....

plant profile

Plant Name:

Botanical Name:

Supplier:

annual ⬜   biennial ⬜   perennial ⬜

Location:

Fertilizer/Soil:

Pest/Weed Control:

flower ⬜   herb ⬜   fruit ⬜   vegetable ⬜   shrub ⬜   tree ⬜

Bloom/Harvest:

Pruning:

Transplant/Propagate/Divide:

Full ⬜   Partial ⬜   Shade ⬜

Size at maturity:

plant notes

plant profile

Plant Name: _____

Botanical Name: _____

Supplier: _____

annual ⭘   biennial ⭘   perennial ⭘

Location: _____

Fertilizer/Soil: _____

Pest/Weed Control: _____

flower ⭘   herb ⭘   fruit ⭘   vegetable ⭘   shrub ⭘   tree ⭘

Bloom/Harvest: _____

Pruning: _____

Transplant/Propagate/Divide: _____

Full ⭘   Partial ⭘   Shade ⭘

Size at maturity: _____

_____

plant notes

....

....

....

....

....

....

....

....

....

....

....

....

plant profile

Plant Name:
_____

Botanical Name:
_____

Supplier:
_____

annual ◯   biennial ◯   perennial ◯

Location: _____

Fertilizer/Soil: _____

Pest/Weed Control: _____

flower ◯   herb ◯   fruit ◯   vegetable ◯   shrub ◯   tree ◯

Bloom/Harvest: _____

Pruning: _____

Transplant/Propagate/Divide: _____

Full ◯   Partial ◯   Shade ◯

Size at maturity:
_____

_____

plant notes

plant profile

Plant Name:

Botanical Name:

Supplier:

annual ◯ biennial ◯ perennial ◯

Location:

Fertilizer/Soil:

Pest/Weed Control:

flower ◯ herb ◯ fruit ◯ vegetable ◯ shrub ◯ tree ◯

Bloom/Harvest:

Pruning:

Transplant/Propagate/Divide:

Full ◯ Partial ◯ Shade ◯

Size at maturity:

plant notes

....

....

....

....

....

....

....

....

....

....

....

plant profile

Plant Name:

Botanical Name:

Supplier:

annual ⬯   biennial ⬯   perennial ⬯

Location:

Fertilizer/Soil:

Pest/Weed Control:

flower ⬯   herb ⬯   fruit ⬯   vegetable ⬯   shrub ⬯   tree ⬯

Bloom/Harvest:

Pruning:

Transplant/Propagate/Divide:

Full ⬯   Partial ⬯   Shade ⬯

Size at maturity:

plant notes

....

....

....

....

....

....

....

....

....

....

....

plant profile

Plant Name: _____

Botanical Name: _____

Supplier: _____

annual ⬜   biennial ⬜   perennial ⬜

Location: _____

Fertilizer/Soil: _____

Pest/Weed Control: _____

flower ⬜   herb ⬜   fruit ⬜   vegetable ⬜   shrub ⬜   tree ⬜

Bloom/Harvest: _____

Pruning: _____

Transplant/Propagate/Divide: _____

Full ⬜   Partial ⬜   Shade ⬜

Size at maturity: _____

_____

plant notes

....

....

....

....

....

....

....

....

....

....

....

plant profile

Plant Name:

_____

Botanical Name:

_____

Supplier:

_____

annual ◯   biennial ◯   perennial ◯

Location: _____

Fertilizer/Soil: _____

Pest/Weed Control: _____

flower ◯   herb ◯   fruit ◯   vegetable ◯   shrub ◯   tree ◯

Bloom/Harvest:

_____

Pruning:

_____

Transplant/Propagate/Divide: _____

Full ◯   Partial ◯   Shade ◯

Size at maturity:

_____

_____

plant notes

....

....

....

....

....

....

....

....

....

....

....

....

plant profile

Plant Name:

_____

Botanical Name:

_____

Supplier:

_____

annual ☐   biennial ☐   perennial ☐

Location: _____

Fertilizer/Soil: _____

Pest/Weed Control: _____

flower ☐   herb ☐   fruit ☐   vegetable ☐   shrub ☐   tree ☐

Bloom/Harvest: _____

Pruning: _____

Transplant/Propagate/Divide: _____

Full ☐   Partial ☐   Shade ☐

Size at maturity: _____

_____

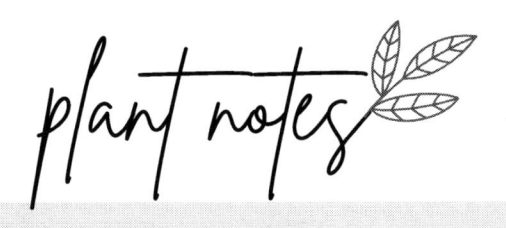

plant notes

....

....

....

....

....

....

....

....

....

....

....

....

plant profile

Plant Name: _____

Botanical Name: _____

Supplier: _____

annual ⭘   biennial ⭘   perennial ⭘

Location: _____

Fertilizer/Soil: _____

Pest/Weed Control: _____

flower ⭘   herb ⭘   fruit ⭘   vegetable ⭘   shrub ⭘   tree ⭘

Bloom/Harvest: _____

Pruning: _____

Transplant/Propagate/Divide: _____

Full ⭘   Partial ⭘   Shade ⭘

Size at maturity: _____

_____

....

....

....

....

....

....

....

....

....

....

....

....

plant profile

Plant Name:
_____

Botanical Name:
_____

Supplier:
_____

annual ⬜   biennial ⬜   perennial ⬜

Location: _____

Fertilizer/Soil: _____

Pest/Weed Control: _____

flower ⬜   herb ⬜   fruit ⬜   vegetable ⬜   shrub ⬜   tree ⬜

Bloom/Harvest:
_____

Pruning:
_____

Transplant/Propagate/Divide: _____

Full ⬜   Partial ⬜   Shade ⬜

Size at maturity:
_____

_____

plant notes

....

....

....

....

....

....

....

....

....

....

....

....

plant profile

Plant Name: _____

Botanical Name: _____

Supplier: _____

annual ⬜ biennial ⬜ perennial ⬜

Location: _____

Fertilizer/Soil: _____

Pest/Weed Control: _____

flower ⬜ herb ⬜ fruit ⬜ vegetable ⬜ shrub ⬜ tree ⬜

Bloom/Harvest: _____

Pruning: _____

Transplant/Propagate/Divide: _____

Full ⬜ Partial ⬜ Shade ⬜

Size at maturity: _____

_____

plant notes

plant profile

Plant Name:
_____

Botanical Name:
_____

Supplier:
_____

annual ⬭   biennial ⬭   perennial ⬭

Location: _____

Fertilizer/Soil: _____

Pest/Weed Control: _____

flower⬭   herb⬭   fruit⬭   vegetable⬭   shrub⬭   tree⬭

Bloom/Harvest: _____

Pruning: _____

Transplant/Propagate/Divide: _____

Full⬭   Partial⬭   Shade⬭

Size at maturity:
_____

_____

plant notes

··

··

··

··

··

··

··

··

··

··

··

··

Made in the USA
Columbia, SC
08 May 2022